Pamela,
May the angels lift you up!
Blessings,

Elin Courter

Angel Blessings Always!

Cassy Tully

Angel Thoughts

Inspiration Peace by Peace

CassyTully

by Elise Cantrell and Cassy Tully

Shining Lotus Publishing books may be ordered through booksellers or by contacting:

Shining Lotus Publishing
418 Tangleridge Dr. Inman, SC 29349
www.shininglotusyoga@gmail.com
www.40DaystoEnlightenedEating.com
1(920) 287-7302
1(920) 917-8562

ISBN: 978-0-9963624-8-1

The authors of this book do not prescribe the use of any advice herein as a form of treatment for physical, medical, emotional or relationship problems without the counsel of a physician, either directly or indirectly. The intent of the authors is only to offer inspiration of a general nature to help you move forward in your quest for body, mind and spirit wellness. In the event that you use the contents and information of the book for yourself, which is your constitutional right, the authors and the publisher assume no responsibility for your actions.

Photo Credits: Mary Holman, Brenda Kay Photography
Back cover photography, Hannah Cantrell Photography
Deanne Schultz, Editor
Tom Rauwerdink, Designer

Printed in the United States of America

Cassy Tully

In dedication and appreciation

Dedicated to my son, Chris, for "moving mountains" and to
miraculous mothers everywhere! To our Divine Creator and
all of the angels and guides who have helped, healed and
inspired us along the journey of life.

Elise Cantrell

Dedicated to my Lord and Savior, Jesus Christ, and my family and friends.
To Elise, for inspiring this book, and my creative team.

You are the angels who have blessed my journey.
It is my hope that this book brings grace and love.

Cassy Tully

Foreword

Finding feathers in our path or noticing sparkles of light are common ways of experiencing angelic presence in our lives. Too often, we overlook these signs, believing angels' divine inspiration and gentle instruction is only for others.

Angel Thoughts: Inspiration Peace by Peace immerses us in the world of angels, where compassionate guidance and soft nudges lead our hearts toward fulfillment and peace.

Cassy's artwork captures the fleeting instance of angels in our lives; paired with Elise's divinely inspired messages, each page celebrates the idea that angelic presence is available to each of us, their graceful creativity working to heal.

CassyTully

Introduction

Elise Cantrell and Cassy Tully wish to share a gift with you: the gift of the angels. Both author and artist have a deep and unique connection to angels. Elise delivers their messages through telepathy and automatic writing, and Cassy connects and shares their images with her pen and paper, paintbrush and canvas. Cassy and Elise realize that the angels move and direct Cassy's art the same way they inspire Elise's words. The angles wish to be seen. They wish to be made known, and they wish to assist us more than ever at this time in history.

The angels brought Elise and Cassy together in friendship with this plan in mind: "You shall bring your light into the world through your sacred sisterhood. You do not have to struggle alone. Even through times of darkness, you are a sacred being of light. Through your friendship, you will heal, open and let the world in. Your sacred relationship nourishes you both into new life, new gifts and new hope. You are helping each other remember how to love and be loved, speak and be heard, see your own true beauty and allow it to be seen in the world. You are supporting each other to let the beauty of your souls be seen."

Now is the time.

Q & A with Elise

Angels

Angels have been known and recognized throughout history in all cultures, creeds, religions and belief systems. They are cited multiple times in holy books including the Bible, Koran, Torah, Buddhist texts, Vedic texts and so on. They have been witnessed throughout cultures all over the world, since the dawn of time. They sometimes come disguised as humans, appear as light, orbs, energy or as human-like beings wearing gowns, halos and wings!

There are many realms of angels, and each angel group has its own specialty. They do not all play harps and fly around in the sky! There are angels of healing, protection, communication, relationships and prayer. There are angels in charge of sound therapy and celestial music. There are archangels, much larger in size, energy and life-force than other realms of angels. There are also "guardian angels," assigned to each person specifically at birth. You do not have to be Catholic to have a guardian angel. We all have them. I am aware that we often actually have more than one. For example, I have three, one male and two female. They each have their own unique personality and energy signature. Each has a special duty or purpose in the care and service of the person they are assigned to. For example, Daniel, my tall, dark-haired male angel, has the strongest presence and is a protective force, offering guidance and warning. I believe he can foresee dangers and help me steer clear. Amy, my blonde female guardian angel, seems to have a practical and teaching approach, keeping me on the right path, always leading me to what I need to know next. Anna, is a shy female guardian angel with long sandy brown hair, small in stature. I believe she prays for my spirit and soul. I have noticed that most people have three angels, but I can't say for sure if this is true for everyone. Some may have more, some fewer.

Angel Communication

Angels are higher-dimensional beings and it requires a high vibrational life-force or state of being to reach the frequency where they communicate. The angels literally down-regulate their vibration while I up-level mine in order to "meet in the middle" so we can communicate with clarity. The best way I can explain it is that we join each other on the same frequency, like talking over a secure channel on a ham radio or a CB. Angels are a bridge between us and God. Because God is of the purest and highest frequency of love and light there is, it is difficult for us to raise our frequency to the level where we can actually hear direct guidance and answers, although at times we certainly can! The lower our energetic vibration, the more difficult it is. God can always hear us and desires to be in contact and connection!

The angels are God's intermediaries, task masters and messengers, helping to put God's will into action, bringing God's messages, answers, solutions, healing, wisdom, love and protection to our level where we can better receive it. We cannot see angels with the human eye because they exist in higher dimensions, specifically the sixth and seventh dimension, while we simultaneously exist in third and fourth dimensions on the earth plane. This is why it is necessary for them to lower their frequency and for us to raise our frequency in order for us to see them and receive their transmissions. We have to find a "radio station" that we can both attune our frequency to simultaneously. They do not have physical bodies, but their energy can take form and matter if necessary, for example, to save us from imminent danger. Many angels do not have a specific gender. They are eternal beings, so procreation is not necessary for their existence. However, they can and do take on a more masculine or feminine energy depending on their assignment.

My Personal Experience with Angel Communication

I've always been a very spiritual and prayerful person, even as a young child. I have experienced endless synchronicities, coincidences and miracles as a result of prayers. As I matured into adulthood and really cleaned up my eating and lifestyle, eliminating impure foods as much as possible, my spiritual connection grew stronger, as if the circuits within me fully connected. I realized I had a gift: I not only had the ability to talk to God, Jesus, angels, Mother Mary, and the Holy Spirit, but they also spoke back, making it possible to have full-blown telepathic conversations. Occasionally, I will actually hear a word or statement in my right or left ear. I think it takes a lot for them to do this, so normally they stick with telepathic communication. They usually do not speak to me in words, but in images and concepts. It is then up to me to translate that into words. It is much like when I was living in France and had to translate between English and French, which eventually became fluid and second nature. Because of my own personal experience, I do not believe you have to be "special" or be a priest or a minister to communicate with heaven. It is there for all of us.

At first, I was reluctant to tell anyone about my experiences, lest I be judged a "nut case," but in recent years I have "come out of the closet," hoping that by sharing my gifts, others will believe in their gifts too. It is said the line between genius and insanity is razor thin, but it is not crazy to speak to your creator and your spiritual allies, it is crazy not to! We can all benefit from the help of God and the angels.

I clearly remember my first incidence of receiving a clear and unexpected message. I was going through a very difficult time and had woken in the night and was lying in bed, restless and anxious, worrying and praying. Suddenly, I heard a voice clearly speaking to me and telling me in no uncertain terms how the situation I was preoccupied with would play out, and that I was not to worry. The situation unfolded exactly as I was told, in a way I could have never come up with myself. From then on, I found these helpful messages would come to me during meditation, prayer, and even randomly during the day or night. Because the first situation played out exactly as I was told, I began to pay attention and take the messages seriously. Over time, I observed that what I was told always became true, and my connection grew clearer and stronger! The angels have put my mind at ease over the years, no matter what hardship I am facing, with their guidance and assurances.

How do I know the messages are coming from Angels?

I am, and have always been, a prayerful person. I pray throughout the day. The messages I get in return are always uplifting, gentle and kind; this is how I know they come from a higher source. I can usually differentiate and identify whether it is God, Jesus, Mother Mary or the angels. They each have a certain "voice" and way of speaking, and their own energy is unique, helping me to identify who is coming through.

In no uncertain terms, I only seek advice that comes from the highest and purest truth, love and light. I do not do séances, use Ouija boards or anything of that nature - EVER! I do not seek to contact ghosts or entities. When I ask for angel messages for myself, my newsletter, or for someone I am helping, I always pray in advance and invite in God, Jesus, the Holy Spirit and the angels in. I always ask to be surrounded and protected by the purest and highest form of love and light. The words of our celestial family always ring of truth, kindness and love, never of manipulation, fear, anger, flattery, confusion, force or telling me that I must do something. Lower entities attempt to use flattery, manipulation and fear as tools of operation, so those should always be a red flag! Angels do not usually foretell the future, but they do try to help you make choices that align you with the highest outcomes and the best possible future. Angels gently encourage and guide. They do not tell us what to do because they respect our free will, and do not want to alter our course in a way that is enabling or that keeps our soul from learning what we came to Earth school to learn. We came here to grow, expand and evolve, and that requires not having all the answers. Angels gently steer, but do not take control or give away the answers to the test of life. Like the kind and loving teachers that they are, they help lead us to find the answers for ourselves. This is for our own highest good.

Can anyone connect with the angels?

I believe we all have this gift of talking to God and the angels, but the subtle voices of these loving beings are easily obscured and overpowered by louder, attention-grabbing distractions like television, smartphones, computers, tablets, video games, drama, conflict and so on. In addition, our access to the frequencies or "channels" from which they communicate are put out of reach by things like ingesting toxic food, excessive alcohol, street drugs, cigarettes, poor lifestyle, environmental pollutants, exposure to toxic household items, mercury, fluoride, pharmaceutical drugs, etc. These things damage our internal receptors. Although messages have come through throughout my life, I never had the clarity I have now until I cleaned up my eating and lifestyle.

The purer we are of mind, body and spirit, the clearer our connection. These high vibrational beings are drawn to high vibrational people. Like attracts like and you attract what you are! The more positive, kind and loving you are, the more likely these heavenly beings are to connect with you. These beings steer clear of dark or unsavory energy just like we steer clear of thugs on the street.

Sometimes the angels will bring forward loved ones living or deceased. I have never tried to make this happen at all, but when it does, and it has happened unexpectedly many times, I trust the angels to keep the space safe and secure, and that this connection is needed for healing.

The angels have promised me that they will never bring anyone to me who I cannot help, so I trust that I can help someone when they come to me, for if not, the angels would have sent them elsewhere. People seem to find me in unusual ways. This is the work of the angels! The angels have promised me that they will never allow someone to come to me who means harm. However, they do seem to love to bring people that will push me further and force me to open, grow and develop my spiritual gifts and talents in new and different ways. I work for God and the angels here on earth, so I guess you could call me an "Earth angel." This is the title I feel most resonates with who I am. There are many of us out there who have volunteered in our own way and with our own distinctive gifts to be the "boots on the ground" in order to assist, help, guide and heal. Just because I do this work doesn't mean my life has been a bed of roses! I am on a spiritual path too, here for soul growth. My own personal struggles and challenges have helped to increase my understanding and compassion for those who come to me for spiritual advice or guidance. This is the first time I have spoken so openly about this work, so it feels a bit risky and I do feel vulnerable sharing, but if my insights help others come closer to God and the angels, then it is worth it.

Many blessings,
Elise

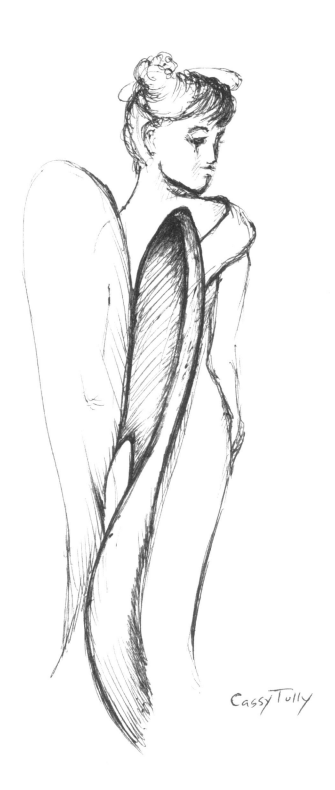

Cassy Tully

Miracle

New Beginnings

It is time to bring to a close any unfinished business left over from previous months. Tie up loose ends and lay to rest anything that no longer brings you to life. Part ways now with that which has served its purpose and played itself out. Put last year's stories behind you. Make way for the new energy that is coming forward. It is an energy of uplifting and renewal. Sacred healing and positive change are at hand. The real you wants to come out of hiding and take over. What you once thought was the real you no longer exists. This forthcoming energy brings greater clarity and discernment than ever before about what you want and what is not for you any longer. Follow the energy and trust that the path will unfold.

How long have you put yourself on the back burner? What inspires you? What empowers you? What have you been longing for that you have been denying yourself from having or being? What are you willing to see now, that you were previously blind to? Are you ready for a fresh start?

Follow where the real YOU leads. You are your own master. Step into self-trust. Stop ignoring your own intuition and your powerful awareness. Stop solely listening to and believing in conditioned, rational thinking that has long kept you stuck in the ordinary when you were meant for the extraordinary! Your uniqueness and potency are much needed. Walk in to the truest version of yourself, give that YOU a hug and say to yourself, "I am finally here." Welcome home, for you have arrived.

It is time to construct the new reality you have been waiting for. Each of you is the artist, architect and builder of your own life, and also the builders of the earth plane that you desire. You are either building or you're not. You are either creating or you're not. Will you settle for the default pattern, or will you create the life, reality and future that you truly desire?

What will you bring into being, and what is ready to crumble? You are beginning the process of renovating not only your own life, but also the world in which you live. Previous months were times of destruction, setbacks and crumbling of the old. Many of you saw a collapse of your former way of life, living and being. Cling no more to what was. It is time to build something new and something greater. Use the "rubble" and "ruins" left behind to build an entirely new and different structure. A new world, the heaven on earth that you are here to bring into being. Although at first it may seem as if each of you are building separately, you are all actually working together to create the new matrix of your world. Each of you intuitively knows your unique task, and as you set about it, you will begin to observe how each of the threads weave together in perfection as if divinely guided. This is because as you follow your own divine guidance individually, the entire fabric of your reality is, indeed, divinely created.

We are excitedly anticipating the beauty that will come from your new creation. This is a time of renewal and reformation. Upgrade your life, living, and being from its former status now. Open and allow something better to come to you and through you. Dream a new dream. Although this project is only in the beginning phases, and is quite expansive, it is time to build the platform and foundation of the beauty that is to come. This energy will amplify your own creative energy. It is a time of starting anew on every level after the collapse of the old paradigms of the last few years.

This is a time of rebirth and resurrection. Nothing can be the same with your newfound perspectives and your new way of looking at the world. But you wouldn't want back those old perspectives now, not after how far you have come. Your hardships have helped you to recognize and step into your talents and strengths and newfound courage and empowerment. Allow that force to move you forward in your new direction.

There is nothing to fear. We are with you every step of the way. You only must begin. As you rebuild, start with the foundation, and carefully place one stone at a time, using love as your mortar, creating something that is sturdy and stable, the "Christ-al" Palace that you have long awaited. That is all that is asked of you here. This is only the beginning, but a beginning it is. Proceed slowly, with grace, trusting your heart's desires, and the rest will come together on its own. And so it is.

As you coast forward, it is important for us to remind you that in order to build and create the reality you choose, you cannot remain in the passenger's seat. It is time to take action now. A new way of living and being is not built on wishes and hopes. It is built by taking action.

You can no longer stand aside and allow things to unfold as they will, or you will not be happy with the results. You have already tried taking a passive role and it hasn't worked. You have primarily been a player in this game called life; now is the time to become the game designer and developer. You have the power to write the program, game plan and playbook. It is time to begin consciously choosing the reality you desire. If you want happiness to show up, you must write it into the framework. You must put a structure in place to support the vibration of happiness. If you are not in a happy place, begin to design the framework of happiness by choosing to add new elements of happiness into your existence, moment by moment, day by day, and happiness will begin to build into your reality. In order to get happiness, you must deliberately invite it in. As a player of the game, you only await the possibility of happiness to show up. As the designer of the game, you write the happiness, healing and peace into the program. It no longer serves you to sit back and wait for your desires to come to you by default. What can you do or be today that will allow happiness to begin to show up right away?

With this new awareness, you can carefully cultivate and curate the reality you wish to inhabit. Write into being the desires of your heart, and they are quickly realized. They are not the mirage...the old default reality is the illusion. Do not settle for the delusion and distortion you have been duped into choosing. Your power as the master of your reality has long been subverted. Activate your latent abilities to develop and design your world the way you desire it to be. As you actively set up the "game plan" yourself, you create new opportunities to come out the winner. Old programming has kept you locked into the player mode, endlessly repeating the same algorithms. You are no longer the chess piece being moved around the board in an eternal match. You can switch roles now and become the one moving the pieces on the board however you want. When you do this, victory is finally at hand.

cassy Tully

Change

You may be noticing many changes occurring right now, all around you in your own life and in your world. Changes in jobs, relationships, people moving to new locations, or even loved ones moving beyond this world and passing over. Know that people who have transitioned in recent years have chosen to do so in order to help, joyfully support, and assist their loved ones with the many challenges and changes the world is experiencing from the other side, where they are not limited by human form.

You may have experienced unexpected losses, chaos, or upheaval in recent times. Perhaps you are being led to make changes in your life, large or small, or have recently experienced some big changes. Perhaps you are feeling inspired to make changes in your diet, lifestyle, living environment, location, relationships, or career. You may be discovering new interests, new skills, new gifts, new motivations, and higher ways of being.

We wish to comfort you by letting you know that all these blessed changes are occurring to align you with new, lighter energies that are becoming available on planet Earth. All these changes serve your highest good, and everything is working out according to plan. You are safe, all is as it should be, and all is well. The less you resist change, the easier your transition to these higher energies will be. You are moving into the age of grace.

You are on the verge of a new dawn. But first, you must walk through the sunset. Before every new beginning, that which existed before must come to an end. Endings are often bittersweet. This is why the fond memories go with you. The longer you spend bidding farewell to what is no longer for you, the further you delay the sweetness of of the sunrise. Do not stay lost in the dark, but follow the light that is guiding you forward, the light of your soul's longing.

You do not have to see clearly what is at the end of the road in order to take a step forward. Step forward in faith. Step by step, the path appears. The path isn't clear because it has never existed before. Your path is unique. You did not choose the well-traveled, worn-out path, but instead came here to pave a new way. You came here to create something that hasn't existed until now. That something is much-needed here in your world. This is your assignment, and your project alone. You have a sense of what that is, but a great deal still remains cloudy and unknown. Each step in faith will move you out of the dense fog and toward increased clarity. When you faithfully move in the right direction, you cannot help but reach your. destination. Each step forward will appear as a building block toward what you came here to manifest.

It doesn't matter that you do not know exactly what you are setting out to create, because one block at a time, the vision will build itself. The mystery of life is in the unknowing, yet trusting and following your own truth and your own awareness toward your soul's calling. Know that you are always being gently guided and led, loved and supported, but the choice to move forward is yours alone.

We understand that many of you are feeling overwhelmed and distressed by the recent storms, hurricanes, earthquakes, fires and floods. Since your outer world is always a reflection of your inner world, we are aware that many of you are now walking through fires of your own as well.

Remember, you are never walking through the fires of life alone. Just like the Biblical story of the three men thrown into a fiery furnace for three days, protected by the angels, you, too, shall come through these trying times, not only unscathed but more empowered than ever before. You will be guided and protected through the fires of life and come through them transformed!

Symbolically, fires are always about transformation, water is always about cleansing, and winds are always about sweeping things out, moving things forward, and bringing about change. The world around you is being changed, cleansed and transformed because it cannot remain as it is and continue on.

Now is the time to place courage above fear, allow peace to expand in your hearts above worry, and inner strength to triumph over victimhood and self-pity. You have the power to find serenity and stillness even amidst the turmoil, trials, and tribulations. When we transform ourselves by finding peace within and being the calm eye at the center of the storm, we then transmute it to the world. As within, so without. As you go, so goes the world. Embodying serenity during turbulent times is your deepest and highest work.

You are standing at a doorway. The door isn't locked; will you go through? The "comfortable" doesn't feel so comfortable anymore, signaling to you it is time to do something different. It is time to take that next step. Before you enter, purge, and bring only what is necessary. Now is the time to lay down your fears, doubts, worries. Stop carrying the heaviness with you.

What are you clinging to that is keeping you from moving forward? What are you willing to shed to enter unencumbered? If you are willing to live on a higher plane, you cannot bring the lower with you. The universe is inviting you to up-level. Have you been ignoring the call, or pretending not to hear? We are gently reminding you that you have chosen a higher path. What lies before you is exactly what you have been asking for, showing up in unexpected ways.

What you leave behind cannot compare to the new treasures you are about to discover. What will you choose?

Like the ebb and flow of tides, ups and downs are a part of life. Instead of swimming against the current, surrender to God and your ship will be carried safely through the storms. By the power of LOVE, your challenges will be transformed into miracles. Your own transformations are gifts to positively influence and inspire others. Your struggles and challenges move you and improve you in ways that make you an even greater gift to all. When you are in alignment with the divine will, all of life becomes miraculous. All will be well as long as you allow the "magic" of divine love to work in you and through you.

Ready, set....reset! What may seem to you like an upheaval in your life or world is actually happening to bring you back to a clean slate, like rebooting a computer. God and the universe are pressing your reset button to prepare you for something new and greater to arise within you and around you. Remember that when rebooting a computer, a "shut down" is required. This is a time to be still, collect yourself, and clear your head. This is not a time of doing, but a time to surrender and BE! Steer away from drama, making big commitments or any other distractions that keep you from moving forward. Please pay heed to the "red flags" we are placing in front of you to steer you in the right direction! Don't over think things. Let your current problems and challenges solve themselves without your further complicating them. Set down your life's questions, trusting that help, answers and solutions will emerge in the stillness, not in struggle and desperation. In this resting space between the old and the new, more will be revealed to you than you can possibly find by your own effort. We are lovingly supporting you through a great time of soul growth. This is a time to keep positive, and stay in gratitude for all that is "right" with your life and with your world, rather than focusing on your angst, tribulations or fears. All the positive forces in the universe respond in kind to appreciation, gratitude and praise. Your thoughts and words are seeds that germinate and plant themselves into your reality. Use the creative power of positivity in your life and in your world and all will be well.

You are reminded during these times to lean not unto your own understanding, but to trust the Lord with all your

Change

hearts. What appears at the outset as disasters, cataclysms and upheaval, is actually things being ordered in new and better ways. Old structures must fall in order for something greater to be created and built in their stead. Things in your world cannot remain as they are. Renewal has begun. We ask you to remain a pillar of strength, hope and faith for others. The dress rehearsal is over and it is time to put into action all that you have practiced and learned. The time is now, and your mission is this: remember your own peace, remember your own faith, remember your own compassion and remember your own light. Remember you are love. By finding strength and hope within yourself, you will show others how to find it within themselves. It is time to forgive, it is time to love without condition, it is time to come together in new ways. Hold unwavering peace in your hearts and give your hearts over to love. By doing this, you will shine great healing light out into the world.

It is time to step back, rest, and receive in order to prepare you for the great things in the works for you. God has planned for you a magnificence beyond what you can imagine. Get ready to open to this new energy advancing toward you now. When these new blessings appear, don't allow fears, doubts or naysayers to cause them to pass you by. You can choose to resist it or receive it. Stay open; this next stage of being may not look the way you imagined, because the energy coming has never before existed. Prepare yourself now for the wonderful things to come. Get ready to be amazed!

This is a time of breakthroughs! The old energy has been clearing out and finally you have moved into a new cycle! This is a time of releasing everything that belongs to the past. Put your challenges and struggles behind you. Release old patterns, wounds, and mistakes that try to dictate your present and future. Breathe a sigh of relief, as all of the personal drama and turmoil is beginning to dissipate. It is in your rear-view mirror, so to speak. You have grown, evolved and up-leveled spiritually through these experiences. Now is a time

to let the lessons settle in so you can absorb everything you have learned. You and your family are protected and safe, and your health, home, vehicles, finances, and dear ones near and far are all being guarded over by God's Holy angels.

If you are in the midst of experiencing a total paradigm shift, where something was different than it seemed, or something didn't turn out the way you had hoped, take heed. In order to transform the situation in a way that will serve you best, it is time to stop planning, scheming or strategizing about how to work the situation out. This will actually work against you right now. There is a time to act and a time to allow grace to take the wheel. Now is the time to let a higher power take over. "Man plans, and God laughs."

"Let go, and let God" with this situation, and you will navigate through it with much more ease as you are moved and directed towards the highest possible outcome. Ask for the miracles that God has set aside for you. God will create a winning strategy if you ask for assistance. It is time to step aside and allow for Divine assistance to take over rather than forcing your plans! Do not force anything at this time. This is a time to let go and trust the will of God to take over.

For everything there is a season. As you are nearing the completion of a project, cycle, relationship or lesson, in order to move forward, you must practice radical acceptance that things have unfolded according to divine plan. Surrender to God. Trust in divine healing. Practice self-care and self-compassion. Allow time for reflection. Tie up all loose ends and bring this assignment to completion so you can move forward, unencumbered, into life's next phase. Make way for all the blessings waiting to flow to you with grace as you step into your "new shoes." Allow divine order to take the lead. Miracles will show up as if right on time. Trust in the ease of synchronicity. Synchronicity floats on the current of grace. Synchronicity is a divine message that you are where you need to be, right on time!

cassyTully

Dance with Wonder

Just as the angels appeared to herald the birth of Christ, so, too, are you "earth angels," here to herald the second coming. You are the trumpets sounding. Many of you are looking for Christ to return before your eyes, but in fact, the Savior is coming through your hearts. As Christ taught, the kingdom of God is within you!

You are here to usher in Christ-consciousness in a way that has never existed before on earth. You show the way. Like fractals of light, you are rays of the "SON."

Many souls are lost and confused, depending on you to show the way. Greener pastures await. It is you who are here to bring other souls to a higher level of living, thinking and being. You are here to usher in "heaven on earth," the "kingdom come" that is answered prayer and prophecy fulfilled. Now is the time.

This is no easy task, as you are well aware. Sometimes, however, you make it harder than necessary. For you do not have to fight against the old ways or the darkness for this new WAY to exist. Instead, you point to the light, bringing it into being, just by being you. By taking a "Christ-like" approach to higher being, you show others the way. Christ was one, but you are many, scattering the seeds of consciousness. We repeat, you ARE the rays of the "SON." Each of you touch countless lives and countless hearts with your own Christ light. "Who am I to be like Christ?" you ask. We reply, "Who are you not to be?" For all were created in this same image and likeness, but most have forgotten who they truly are and where they came from. Now is the time to reclaim your inheritance, the birthright that has been obscured from you for so long.

You are mistaken in your belief that you have to be perfected in order to complete this task, or to do God's work. This is what you've been told, but nothing could be further from the truth. The only requirement is to have a willing heart and the courage to serve. The idea that one must be without a flaw,

mistake, or sin in order to be of service has only halted the progress of you and your planet for generations, hindering you from giving birth to this new world. This point of view has held in place a lower, denser frequency of fear, guilt and shame, rather than the lightness of non-judgment, forgiveness and unconditional love that were the teachings of Christ.

Christ came to remind you that you are guiltless in the eyes of God. His message has been misconstrued and deconstructed as a means of control, holding you prisoner to a worn out paradigm by the shackles of your sins, guilt and mistakes. Christ came to remind you that as a child of God, you are already free. Just as your own children are most loved despite their flaws, errors and mistakes, as a child of a loving God, it can be no other way for you. Throw down your guilt, suffering, and burdens at the feet of Christ so that you may get about the task of ushering in God's kingdom, a new earth. Stop wasting your energy on guilt and fear, and redirect those energies into the power of love. Now is the time, and you are the way. Christ will be born again on Christmas through YOU, and indeed shall return!

Many of you reading this message are yourselves angels. We admire and applaud you as the most courageous and fearless of the angel tribe. You have our greatest respect. For you have chosen to physically embody on the earth plane in order to appear in the right place at the right time. You are often called "an angel" by those whose paths you cross. You are the boots on the ground. Angelic traits are encoded into your DNA. You are hardwired to be sensitive, intuitive, compassionate and empathic. You are natural helpers, healers, nurturers and light warriors. You give without thinking. Your actions themselves are answers to prayers, and you pray yourselves without ceasing. You are a LIVING prayer. You are LOVE in action. You are always there to uplift, encourage and inspire. You sense and relieve suffering by nature. It is YOU whom we are here to support. You are hands and hearts in action, getting your hands "dirty" because you roll up your sleeves and do the hard work. You remind people that goodness exists.

We remind you again that only the most courageous of the angelic realm have chosen to incarnate on the earth plane. Your planet is the most dangerous, hostile and challenging to inhabit in all dimensions throughout the cosmos. It is also the place where the most growth is possible for all beings. You are here to help in that endeavor. You choose to come, yet you were chosen yourselves for your remarkable strength, integrity, kindness, love and resilience of spirit. You will be greatly rewarded for your assignment here in this density at this time in history. We thank you for your service to humanity. We bless you for your dedication to spreading kindness, positivity, light and love.

Stillness

The Way Forward

The way forward is not as hard as you make it out to be. Humans have a tendency to overthink and over-rationalize, keeping them in a holding pattern. The way forward is following the pull. Let yourself be pulled. Yes, there is always an energetic pull guiding you forward and showing you the next step to take. Because it is subtle, and often doesn't match with your conditioned thinking, many ignore and resist the pull. The pull which we are speaking of feels much like the natural current of movement in a stream to where you are going next. Many fight the current, creating struggle, stagnation and lack of progress. The reason you are feeling stuck is because you aren't going with the pull of the natural current.

Yes, changes are afloat, and if you are willing to follow this current of grace, instead of struggling against it, you will arrive with ease. Do not let your fears keep you from the next juncture. Life is about moving forward with steady progress. You cannot do this when you live out of fear. When you fear what lies ahead, you create friction and stagnation. Trusting that what is ahead is right for you is the way to align with the pull, the current of grace that moves you towards your soul's highest destiny.

Yes, you may hit rapids or rough waters from time to time. When this happens, remember the riverbanks guiding your passage are lined with love. The waters that carry you are actually the arms of grace. We, the angels, are your guides. No matter how treacherous the current seems, the journey is always love, and the path always leads back home. You wouldn't have come here if you weren't up for the challenge. Your calling is to be true to your heart. Everything you need to know is written there. What are you waiting for? Jump in and enjoy the ride!

You have been asking how you can serve. You have been hearing a calling within you. Many are called, but few heed the call, and even fewer answer, fewer than those carry out their calling. What are you being called to now? Each of you has a unique calling, and no two are alike. Will you respond?

If not now, when?

God and the angels are waiting for you to take up your calling and follow your path. Many living souls depend on your answer. This world needs you now. If you are waiting for confirmation, waiting for a push, waiting for the right time, waiting for the right conditions, we are here to tell you the time is now. The entire universe is holding its breath, waiting and watching to see if you will follow through with your call to service. The ideas you have been receiving are divinely inspired. The question you must ask is whether you will stay with the comfortable status quo, or step into your calling. The choice is yours. They are two very different paths. It takes great courage to branch out in a new direction. We are patiently waiting for your response.

Now is the time, a final phase of the regeneration and renewal that must occur to allow you to reach new levels of consciousness. Each of you requires something different. Trust that you will be led through this process by your own special team of angels. It is time to "dust off" and clean out the remaining clutter and debris in your inner and outer world. It is a time of going into the far reaches, closed off and forgotten about. If you think you have done a thorough job of purging that which you no longer need, think again. Cobwebs remain. Go deeper, and go further. Go into those darkest and scariest places...the basement and the attic of your heart and mind. There is still much left to be purged hiding in those deepest recesses.

Think of yourself and your life as a remodeling project. One that you have begun, but that is not yet complete. As you begin to remodel, you uncover more and more that needs to be ripped out, repaired or renovated in your life. Leave no corner untouched. Get rid of what is not worth keeping. It will only weigh you down on the path forward. Get ready for new beginnings, new life and new you. The freer and more unencumbered you are, the easier you will launch.

The time is now.

You have been on a long and winding hike through the untamed wilderness and more recently, the journey has been a slow and precarious uphill climb. The journey is not over yet, but you have reached a plateau with a small, quaint village and a cozy inn with a nice place to dine. Do you pass by and keep going, or do you stop to rest before resuming your travels?

If you rest now, you will have what it takes to continue on with courage and zest. As fearless as one must be to embark on an arduous journey, so too must you be fearless enough to pause, rest, and replenish yourself for what comes next. The time to venture on is coming soon.

We use this metaphor to remind you that your earthly life is also a journey. You cannot continue to climb the ladder of eternity without pause and rest. Our message is this: you will get to where you're going more efficiently if you allow yourself needed downtime. Do not be afraid to pause and rest. You must allow yourself time to absorb the teachings and the lessons before moving forward. Assimilate now so you can use the newly acquired knowledge for what lies ahead. Perhaps a rested body and mind will allow you to look at things a little differently, and approach the path with renewed vigor. Perhaps a pause is needed to look at the map and rethink the direction in which you are headed. Perhaps there is a better path. Remember, you are on a journey rather than a race. Pace yourself and it will be more pleasant and delightful. Rest is required, and whenever you arrive, it will be right on time.

We are working with humankind to help you move forward from fears and wounds, past suffering and pain that keeps you in an eternal holding pattern of smallness. You were not created to remain small. Like all of nature, you were created to grow and evolve and become something greater. Some will allow themselves to grow more than others. Some carry deeper wounds. Your deepest wounds can serve as your road map for the very areas you need to grow most. You can let your emotional suffering weaken you or empower you. We want you to realize that what you have survived has strengthened you, not weakened you. We stand in awe of the strength and courage of the human spirit! Can you recognize how strong you really are? Rely on this strength; do not doubt it, for it will propel you further forward than you can possibly imagine.

Trust your inner knowing. Humans have been conditioned to mistrust their own inner truth in deference to what they are told to think. This "brainwashing" is what was meant by the term "false prophets." Your own thinking can present itself as a false prophet if it comes from the conditioned mind and not from the wisdom of your inner voice. Don't be told what to think by the world. God speaks to you from within. That is why Jesus reminded us that "The kingdom of God is within." Do not get confused when the messages you get from the world conflict with the messages coming from your inner wisdom. If the two are incompatible, know the inner voice is always right. That inner voice is the voice of your creator, who always has your best interest, your highest good, in mind. The voice of this world has a false agenda that does not come from your loving God.

We wish to remind you that no bad decision, wrong turn, or mistake ever goes uncorrected in the perfection of creation. There is nothing that can occur to prevent God's plan from coming to pass in divine timing. The momentum of God's will is unstoppable and human mistakes only offer the smallest friction and resistance. All of the pieces will ultimately fall into place. It can be no other way. The only limitations you will ever encounter are those created in your mind. Even those God finds his way around. All is well and all will be well.

Many of you are wondering what the future will bring. Suffice it to say that the future will bring many positive changes into

The Way Forward

the lives of those who are ready to ascend and embrace a higher way of living. You are standing at the dawn of the age of grace, because we are pouring out the cup of grace upon you now. What you do with it is up to you. If you fight, resist, or work against the flow of grace, you will be unable to receive the harmony available to you here and going forward. If you allow grace to settle into you, and you into it, then your life will begin to align in miraculous and beautiful new ways. The world around you will align in glorious ways as well. Everyone is being given an opportunity to rise to a higher plane of existence and higher ways of being, though not all will choose it. We have been preparing you for this new beginning. Get ready to soar!

You find yourselves at a crossroads. It is a crossroads of your belief systems and ways of being. You are at a fork in the road on earth. There are those who are choosing only to serve themselves in this lifetime (the users); there are those who choose to serve others (the givers); and there are those on the fence. You are all being presented with a choice at this time. Energies and events behind the scenes are working to push those who are teetering back and forth out of their selfishness and into love. Darkness is being purged both from you and around you. Current energies are helping keep "you" to overcome fear, blocks and emotional factors that have had negative influences over you, so you can awaken to truths that have been long hidden.

This is a time of great insights about yourself, and awakened awareness of a new way forward. You have already begun to notice a desire to move in a new direction toward something more meaningful. The shallow rewards that once interested you have lost their charm, and it is time to leave the past behind. You have grown spiritually and emotionally, and you yearn for something deeper. The answers are within. You will see that once you find your true path, the blessings and rewards are far beyond the material!

Your challenges allow you to discover the power of your inner strength. You are even stronger than you realize! However, your true strength lies in your capacity for kindness, compassion and unconditional love. Your true strength lies in your ability to forgive, both yourself, and those who have caused you suffering. You have grown greatly from these challenges and life experiences. The more you believe in yourself and find who you truly are beneath the rubbish and false perceptions, the more powerful you are! It is here where your ability to heal, serve, love, forgive and live will reach its full capacity.

Re-attune to the frequency of love. You were created from this vibration but we acknowledge it can be difficult to maintain in the dense energy of your planet. Love wants you back "on-line."

Let yourself be pulled toward love in every way. Love is like a tow boat drawing you back home to shore. Allow it to tow you home to yourself and your natural state of being. As you trust where it is leading you, everything around you begins to change…for the better.

Change is indeed at hand. It is pulling you so strongly that you can no longer resist it. There is nothing to fear. Like gravity, the further away from love you get, the stronger its pull. It is time to move with this force rather than resisting, knowing that this force is grace. Grace wants to move you fully into the love that you are. Grace is always working toward your highest destiny and your true purpose. Grace is always drawing you back home to yourself, closer to the eternal source of love.

If you feel the breath has been knocked out of you from circumstances you have been experiencing, breathe now and allow yourself to be filled with the breath of grace, the breath of God. Let that breath move you, and let it lead you back to your sacred self and toward a future more beautiful than you can contrive. Love wants you happy, love wants you whole, love wants you healed. Love keeps pulling until you arrive. When you live from total love, you are home.

Cassy Tully

The Lesson Is Love

Everything you encounter here in this dimension and density is a lesson in love. You chose to come here to know love in all forms and facets. Your life and your reality is a classroom. Your entire earth experience is filled with tests, challenges and experiments created to encourage you to know all colors, flavors, shapes and sizes of love. There are many chapters in the book of love and many facets, forms, varieties and variations on the theme. The lessons come in many disguises and degrees and descriptions. Once you recognize the lesson is always love, then you no longer resist the teaching. The more completely the lesson is learned, the more quickly one graduates to the next level, and begins the next chapters of learning. The same love lesson often shows up in various appearances, embodiments and structures until you have mastered it.

There are two kinds of love: God's love and your love. As you progress through the lessons and levels, your love becomes a closer reflection of Divine love. As your love becomes a mirror of God's love, you begin to recognize that you and love are one. You are love. If you are love, you have an unlimited capacity to love and be loved. Once you are the purest and clearest reflection of love, you recognize yourself as the same love in the mirror before you. You know who you truly are. You then, in that knowledge, expand that love into all eternity, all universes and all creation. This in itself is your soul's highest destiny...you are designed to discover and become who you already are. LOVE.

Your earth is known as the most advanced school in which love is the primary curriculum. Many of you believe we are here to teach you about love, but you are the ones who help us come to know and understand love. We watch as you tenderly hold a child and rock it to sleep. We see you gaze into the depths of your lover's eyes. We watch you sink to your knees when a loved one is gravely ill. We see your bliss in the embrace of your soulmate. We watch your face light up when a special someone enters the room. We've seen one man take a bullet in order to save his comrades.

We observe as you lean into a friend's suffering, offering to share in the burden, lifting them from despair. We watch you struggle when someone you love struggles. We see you cry because of someone else's tears. We watch you sit at the bedside of an elder, holding their lifeless hand as they pass from the earth plane into eternity. We watch in anticipation as an infant breathes its first breath and is placed in the arms of its overjoyed parents. We look on as you love a stranger by hearing their story and offering assistance, money, or advice as if they themselves were your beloved. We are greatly moved by your love.

We acknowledge that humans have a capacity for love that is even greater than their fear, pain or suffering. You choose love again and again, regardless of of the possibility of disappointment, grief or loss. You give all for love. You will stop at nothing for love. You lose yourself in love. You throw your hearts into situations in which you have everything to lose. The cumulative love on your planet far outweighs dark tendencies. You look to us for advice on love, but it is we who look to you to show us what love truly is. You are here to let love evolve and expand through you, and with it, you too are expanded and evolved. We admire your courage and determination, and refusal to give up when it comes to love. We celebrate love with you. It is you who teach the cosmos. You show the way.

If you are feeling as if you are in a spiritual battle, fear not. Your weapons are simple: holding peace in your heart, stay in a place of gratitude and kindness, exuding love in all you do. This repeals any and all negative spiritual energy. Do not allow yourself to be tricked, fooled or pulled out of the power you have over darkness. Your power is peace, kindness, gratitude and love. With these alone, darkness is defeated!

Be a warrior of the light by expanding the love you hold in

your heart. Stay centered in love in all that you do, and do not let your heart waver from the love zone. By expanding the love zone in your heart, you expand it in the world. Your heart center is a portal that can access the vast and endless amounts of love through all time and space. You can draw abundant love into your life by opening your heart and drawing from the well of love available within you. You can make your entire life a love zone if you choose. Love will guide your heart to live fearlessly.

Let your challenges strengthen you in love, and bring more love into your challenges, and you cannot fail.

Fear and truth are opposing energies. Is fear or truth speaking? Learn to discern between them by listening with your heart. We angels never speak messages of fear, but instead guide you with clarity through the troubled waters you encounter and help you to navigate toward your highest good. We help you see things as they really are, not through the eyes of fear. We are your guides on the path of love. We wish to tell you now that smoother waters are ahead. The tides are finally turning.

We observe you and see many opportunities for generosity that you aren't choosing. We can't help but wonder how much kinder and gentler your world could become if generosity became a constant. Most believe that generosity is only about money and charity, but generosity comes in infinite forms. Small kindnesses, compliments, even a smile, are forms of generosity. Forgiveness is a form of offering generosity that many of you do not recognize! You often hold back from delivering the simplest forms of generosity, thinking monetary giving is greater. Many do not realize that giving is not limited to the material. What can you give to a loved one or even a stranger that won't cost you a thing, but will make their life brighter? What small acts can you choose right now that will bring hope to someone else?

You bless yourself and the world when you present yourself in life with a giving heart. By blessing others, you always bless yourself! The act of giving helps dispel the illusion of lack, poverty or scarcity. Without these fears standing in your way, you open yourself to more abundance. When you refuse to share, you limit yourself from receiving by this mindset. When you forgive another their wrongdoing, you too are released of your own transgressions. Abundance is a way of life that includes the continuous flow of giving, sharing and receiving! Always give thanks when you receive, but don't forget to give thanks that you always have something to give.

Many of you believe that your kindness only helps to improve the lives of others, without recognizing the ways it improves your own! How will you respond to the opportunities around you to give of yourself, and open to receive more in return? Pay close attention to how much more you receive when you align yourself with generosity in all of its forms!

It is impossible to be separated from love, for love always returns to its source. Therefore, you cannot be permanently separated from those you love in life or in death. Love cannot be destroyed. Love is eternal. Love is the underlying principle of all of creation. Love is who you are.

Patience

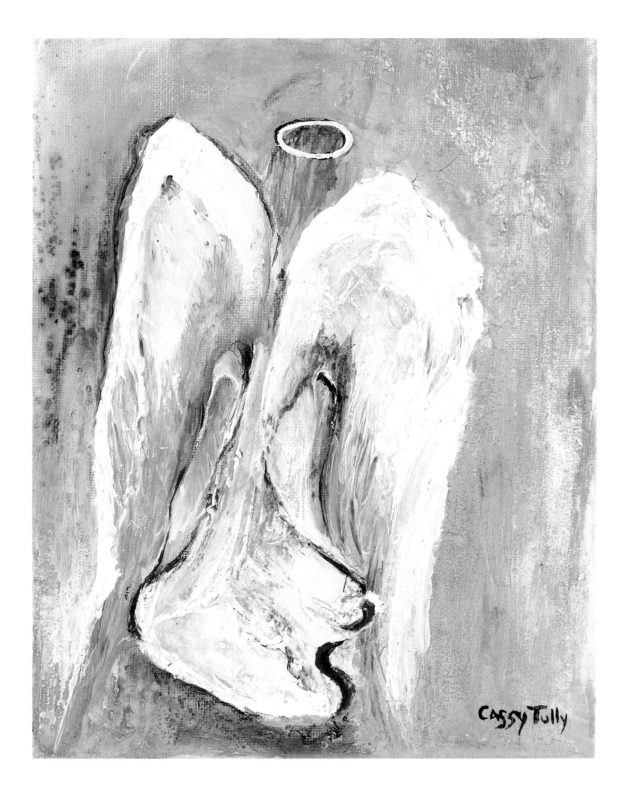

The Power of Transformation

You are the fire of transformation, of healing, of wisdom, of love and of light. You have the ability to transform any situation you face with the light of the fire within. Love is the most powerful fire there is, having the ability to transform everything it encounters. It is only a matter of time. Now is the time to reclaim your power to transform anything that is troubling you into something positive, something higher. Now is the time to practice the art of transformation in your life. What you practice, you eventually master.

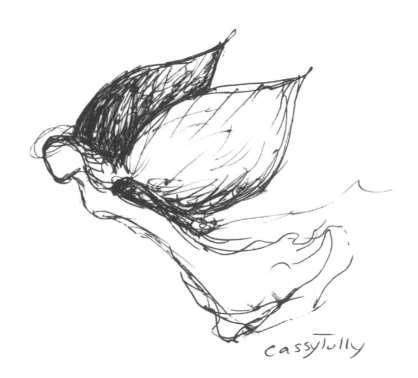

CassyTully

Shine a Light

Breathe. The light is there at the end of the tunnel. You may only see the smallest pinpoint from your current perspective, but it is there and it is growing. As it grows, the light within you grows as well. You and the light are one. The more the light grows in you, the more the light grows and shines in the world.

"What do I have to do to make the world a better place?" you ask.

You are already doing it...being you. The more of YOU that you allow to show up, and the more you choose to align with who you are, the more you align with your life's true purpose, and the brighter a light you become to those around you. Everyone's soul purpose and destiny involves being the light and gift and using your gifts to brighten the world. In its current form, this world values only certain gifts, but you can be sure that all gifts are valuable, necessary and needed, and there are no gifts the Creator values more than any other. Do not leave your gifts on the table. Take them up now. When you reject your gifts, you reject the One who made manifest those gifts within you.

"Who am I to share my gifts?" you ask, as if you are nothing special.

We are here to tell you that everyone who has chosen to incarnate on the earth plane is special. Only the bravest and highest souls apply for this mission, and only the best and brightest are chosen. The entire universe is watching your unfolding and cheering you on. If you only knew that the love and light of eons is right there at your side, and at your beck and call, lending you loving support and guidance, you would realize that nothing you have taken on in this earth plane is impossible. Legions of angels have your back and are leaving you breadcrumbs to show the way, guiding you to the very light at the end of the tunnel that you have been waiting for.

You cannot "lose" yourself, but your true light can get hidden or buried under everything that is not you. Uncover "you" from the "not you." Dust yourself off and stand up and proclaim your wholeness. The only way you can be defeated in life is to reject the gift that you are. Your gift IS your YOUness. The one thing you cannot fail at is being you, unless you refuse it.

Sometimes growth requires you to take action to move up, and sometimes it requires a pause - getting quiet and still to draw in strength and nourishment like a flower bud before it opens. When you become quiet and still like a lake, that which is real and true is reflected more clearly in you, and becomes apparent.

When life requires you to move ahead, it is as if you are climbing a mountain or scaling a wall. One hand must let go and reach up - in order to grip the next rung, the next piece of rope, the next ledge - to pull yourself higher. Climbing from where you are always requires stretching to reach further. Without letting go of where you are, and stretching up, there is no rising. You were made to rise, and all of the forces of nature and the cosmos are supporting your ascension. We, the angels, gently beckon you now to arise. We are the winds of spirit helping you up. We are always assisting your rise!

It is important for lightworkers and earth angels (you know who you are) to find your own tribe and surround yourself with like minds that will inspire you and push you to grow and evolve. You will help each other keep your vibration elevated and your spirits uplifted during trying times. Seek others who reflect your light, bring you good company and bring out your best! You are a great gift to other light beings. You help each other dance on the spiritual path. When you are in a group of high-minded people, you hear the exact words you need to hear, and will receive guidance and confirmation about which step to take and which path to follow.

Spirit speaks in unexpected ways through those who are highly attuned to their creator and aligned with the will of God. You have found your people when you experience radical acceptance among them. Your time together will be harmonious and you will have peace in your heart when they are around. When you have found your tribe, it will feel like you are home.

You came into this world to encourage by your example. Your light came here to shine the way. You didn't come here to fit into this world, you came to change it. We realize your frustration with those who seem blind to the path, do not see, and do not choose to come with you now. We share this frustration. It saddens us that not all are receptive when we are so well-meaning in all we do to help and guide. Just as Jesus stated, "Many are called, but few will answer."

There have been many like you throughout time, lighting the path for others, showing them the way, but at this time, many, many others are present with you, amplifying the positive effects. Together we reach the energetic "tipping point" of love and light, and many more will come on line. We are here assisting this transformation.

Rest assured, your mission is unique to you alone, and you are specially adept and equipped to handle the assignment being asked of you. You will gather and lead those most attuned to your frequency on the soul path and bring them with you, for it is the divine will that not one soul is left behind. Lead gently, yet courageously. Speak the words placed in your heart, and your voice will be a beacon. Your light will brighten many hearts and bring hope.

Each one of you is a "pied piper," gathering all who will come as you lead them home to love, wholeness, and the truth of who they are. As you follow the voice of inspiration, impulse and intuition, which is the whisper of God, you serve the voice of love. You were made to walk and to fly with the angels.

During times when darkness seems thick and dense, the only cure for it is it's opposite: LIGHT.

You are of the light. There is no darkness that light cannot penetrate. Remember, you are a ray of light from the great Source of ALL light. Refuse to let anything come between you and shining bright. As you shine together, the darkness will disappear.

cassyTully

Divine Knowledge

How do you connect with streams of information that belong to the infinite sea of consciousness? It is most accessible through silence, stillness, dreamtime, imagination, meditation, prayer and the relaxed state between wake and sleep.

Divine knowledge is not about learning, but remembering. Consciousness is infinite but you have been conditioned to see only the finite. When you begin to follow your intuition and awareness, rather than the confines of the logical mind, you enter the doorway into the infinite where all wisdom is found, all answers are stored and all solutions await. You have been taught to limit yourself to that which is attained by human learning. Instead, let wisdom teach you. Become open. The rational, logical thinking that is so prized in your world is the false ceiling that limits access to rivers of wisdom. Logic is the cloaking device that has kept infinite truth hidden for generations. Logic encourages limited thinking that blocks access to the unknown, using the illusion of the known to keep divine wisdom just out of reach. We are not saying that logic is bad. It is a necessary thought process in your world in certain situations. However, logic can be a limiting factor when it comes to accessing all other aspects of consciousness, especially those that are not commonly known or yet understood.

Wonder is the vibrational "code" that accesses knowing. When you dance with wonder, consciousness flows. Wonder alone is the frequency needed to connect the circuit between known and the unknown. When Jesus said "you must become like a child, to enter the kingdom of God," He was alluding to curiosity, openness and wonder as a doorway. By thinking you know God, you cannot know him. By stepping into wonder and awe, you discover for yourself. Wonder allows you the opportunity to recognize and remember. Consciousness is where you came from, and consciousness is who you are. Everything else is illusion. Remembering the way IS the way...

Unto you it is given to know the kingdom of God. The kingdom of God lies within you. Everyone is invited, but few accept. Everyone is given the keys, but few choose to enter. The portal to heaven's gate is inside you. When you pray, you access the "inner gate" to the kingdom of God within, through which all blessings flow and spill over into reality. You access God through yourself and your inner pathway. This is how silent prayers reach the ears of God, and this is also how the answers return to you. When you make a prayerful request, God reorders your reality to allow the request to show up. The answer to your prayers comes as unexpected blessings, helping hands, timely advice, sudden insights, new ways of looking at things, aha moments, angels in disguise, unfolding miracles, coincidences, synchronicities, and inner knowing. As these show up, know that God is there, and God is behind them. Take a deep breath right now, knowing that the highest angels and guides are lined up and ready to answer your call. They will show you the way, they will fine tune the details, and they are at your service to make sure that everything turns out according to divine plan. Your journey will be filled with enchantment, blessings, and miracles if you invite them along! All you need is to do is ask and your joy may be full. And so it is!

CassyTully

cassyTully

Peace

You do not find peace. Peace is who you are. You were created by peace and for peace. When you are not at peace, it is because you are allowing the chaos of the world to pull you out of who you are. You are believing the world rather than believing the truth that is always there inside of you.

How do you prevent turmoil, fear and chaos from pulling you our of your natural state of peace?

We want to tell you that anything that doesn't come from love is a distortion, a lie. When you put your beliefs in these, they grow in strength. When you put your beliefs in love, that grows in strength. Be especially conscious of where you are focusing your energy and attention right now. There are those who do not wish for you to know peace. There are those who wish to lure you away from the path of love, and they will use any means to do just that. Anything that comes from a fear-based energy or mentality is an attempt to pull you out of the peace that you are. You are being tricked into delusion.

Pay attention to what causes you to lose your peace, and begin to consciously eliminate it from your life and your reality, finding things of a peaceful nature to replace that. For example, your news media is designed to keep you angry, confused and in fear and chaos. This is a form of mind control that is being weaponized against human kind. We want to make you aware, so that you do not let outside forces hijack you from your natural state of peace. You cannot be manipulated from a place of peace. You can only be manipulated from a state of fear and confusion. And you are being manipulated right now indeed, as a collective.

We ask you now to return to peace by mindfully turning away from that which steals your peaceful presence. Many of you are so used to being in a heightened state of alert, and a heightened state of fear, that you have forgotten what peace feels like. You have forgotten that it is possible. You have forgotten that is who you are. Instead, you live life like a frightened animal, reacting unskillfully from a place of fear instead of a place of knowing, which comes from existing in your natural state of peace. The time is now to return to your peace. The time is now to come home to love.

Strength

CassyTully

Zero Point

A portal of energy has opened with the passage of the equinox, and you have now entered a window of time-space we call zero point. Zero point is an intersection of time-space in which all possibilities are opened to you. In quantum physics, this is called the source field. This opportunity is a convergence of time-space that allows you to merge with Source, God, or the Creator. It can allow the very energy that created universes to flow through you now, to recreate your own universe, or the reality in which you live. You are the architect and builder of your own universe, life or reality and it is time to remodel, update, and redesign it however you choose. Your life, your reality, doesn't happen to you, it happens through you! Now through early next year, the time is ripe to examine your opportunities, belief systems, dreams and desires. Previously you have been creating your reality from past templates, repeating the same mistakes time and time again. These old templates come from past human templates, passed on for eons with the same patterning that leads to failure and destruction. Now is the time to rewrite your script and thus rewrite the script for humanity. Review, reexamine, and rebuild your life template and your current state of being into that which you truly desire.

Clarify what you would like to create by asking questions about what you wish to have now, what needs to go, and what you would like to change. What new possibilities want to present themselves at this opportunistic point in time? What would you like to see take place now and in the future? Due to profound spiritual growth, your point of view has significantly shifted, and your priorities have significantly reordered. It is time to overhaul, renovate, and redesign your life, your template, from the ground up (zero point) however you want. Listen to your inner guidance, your inner wisdom, and your innermost desires in order to create what is next. In the past, you have been misguided and pressured to create what others want, but this time around, it is most important that you create what you want. Remember this is YOUR reality, not someone else's! Because you are in this source field,

your dreams and desires are most in alignment with that of the Creator. Previously, you have been misdirected by other forces that do not have your best interest in mind, but their own. Trust your own inner compass. Trust your instincts and your own awareness to be accurate and right for you, for they are truly messages from the One from which you were made. They are most in alignment with the Creator's template for your life. Here is your chance to create the life you have always wanted, most in alignment with your highest good, and to design your own reality as if you were building your dreams! The time is now!

Nothing in your time-space reality is linear. Linear thinking is a grand illusion. When you think only in linear terms, you limit yourself. Everything in the Universe expands outward from a central point, including you. Your soul's growth is not linear, it is expansive.

Just as humans have a physical growth spurt, you also have soul growth spurts. When you experience a soul growth spurt, you may need more sleep, rest, reflection, solitude and silence. You may occasionally experience some growing pains associated with your soul growth, but as with physical growing pains, they will pass and quickly be forgotten.

Your soul was born into this world to up-level. Higher aspects of yourself are always emerging and evolving. Trust the process, and trust that you are always supported and never abandoned by God and the angels, even in the darkest hours. Challenges and struggles allow you to develop and master parts of yourself to take quantum leaps forward in your soul's learning process. Everything is built into your soul's journey to empower and expand you. Just as the universe is ever expanding, so are you. Breaking through obstacles allows you to realize your true strength and deepens your faith in yourself and in God.

Cassy Tully

cassy Tully

The Three Ps

We ask you to use this time to reflect on the Three Ps: Purification, Priorities and Purpose. Many of you are feeling like you are drowning in confusion, so focusing on these three areas will bring clarity.

Purification: it is time to re-evaluate your life right now. What was working for you before may no longer work in your favor now as you emerge from a period of soul growth. What do you need to clear our of your life in order to purify so you can become a clearer channel of love and light?

Priorities: Reflect on your true priorities. Things might have shifted for you, and what was once important to you may no longer take precedence. It may be time to let some things go to honor the new order of things. Ask what is right for you now. What areas of life do you need to place the most focus and energy on to enact the future you wish to create? Where is the greatest contribution of your time and energy?

Purpose: Did you come to serve self or others? It is time to own and activate your passions, gifts and talents in such a way that allows you to fulfill your soul's highest destiny. What you choose today will create what arrives in the future. No more spinning your wheels in the endless cycle of doubt and fear. The time is now. Step forward with an open heart and trust yourself to be divinely guided in baby steps towards your mission, your magic and your soul's true purpose.

Advice from Archangel Michael

Always be honest with yourself. Facing the truth takes courage. You must first acknowledge what is there in order to change or heal it. Admitting the truth is often what it takes to get unstuck and take positive action.

Be kind to yourself. Most humans would never dare treat others as harshly as they they treat themselves. Be gentle and nurturing to yourself as if you were your own child, for you are a child of God. Treat yourself the way you desire others to treat you.

Make your health a priority. Direct your actions in ways that nourish and support your wellbeing. Notice the areas where you are sabotaging your health. You were created to be healthy and whole. Your physical health allows you to carry out your divine life purpose.

Challenging situations in life are always moving towards resolution. Many problems solve themselves if you let them. Stop adding to your problems and overcomplicating them by adding fear to the equation. Fear always causes you to react unskillfully, to make choices that add further injury to an unpleasant situation. Give your concerns to God and the angels, and in return you will experience divine peace. Everything is always working towards your highest good. Trust that all of the powers of the universe are working in your favor.

Forgive yourself. Guilt holds you hostage to the past by negative judgments directed inward. It keeps you small, afraid and unworthy. Release all judgment and criticism of yourself in order for your soul to expand. Every child of God is worthy. Self-forgiveness allows you to move forward in peace.

Pray for help! Don't hesitate to ask for divine help, intervention and miracles. When you do this, you will be offered helpful guidance, insight and grace to ease your burdens and assist with challenging situations. Often, God doesn't snap His fingers and make your struggles disappear, but instead guides you through them with clarity and grace. Once you come through life's struggles, you will learn and grow. If your struggles haven't catalyzed you to grow in divine grace and love, then God's work is still in the process of being completed in you.

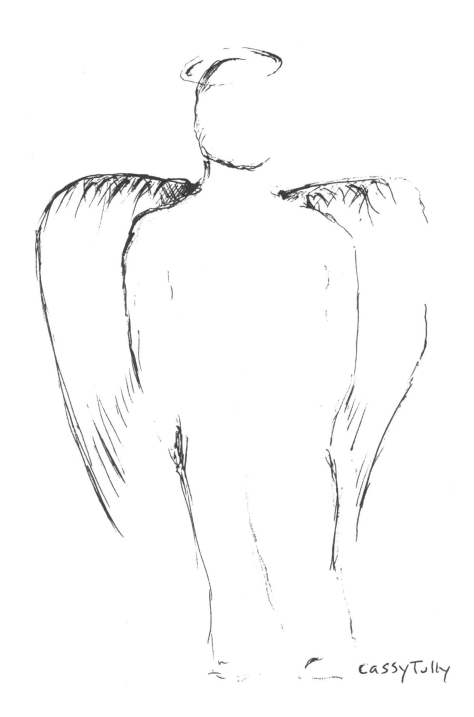

cassyTully

Hope

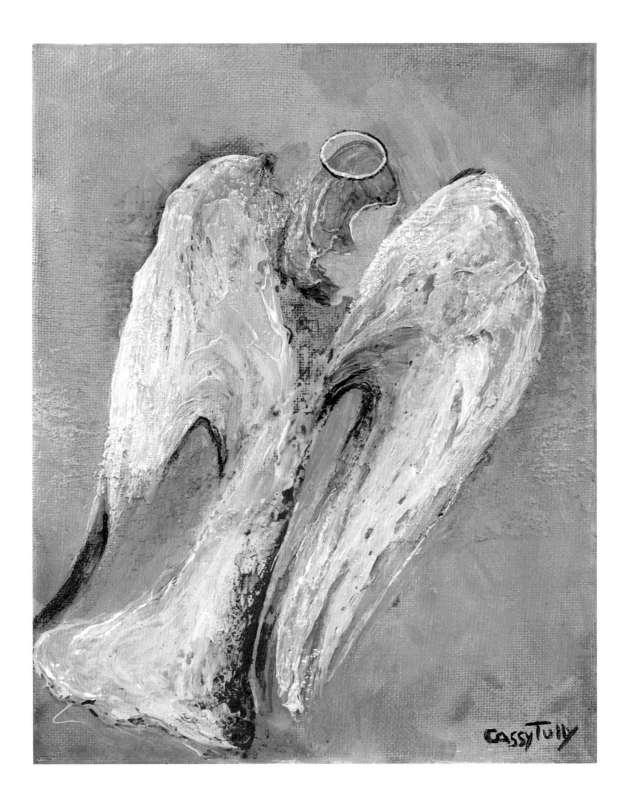

CassyTully

Inspired by Jesus

Jesus spoke of the "eye of the needle" that you go through in order to ascend to God's kingdom. Another way to look at it is a "birth canal." You transition out of the world the same way you came in. Through this narrow "birth canal," all that can come into this world and leave this world is the true YOU. As you go out, nothing or no one can come with you except the growth, wisdom, truth and love you found while on the earth plane. These are the only things that can be accumulated in eternity. These alone are truly yours. Carefully curate what you choose to accumulate while you are here. Place your energy only on the riches that can come with you.

Blessed are the peacemakers for I work through them and I am with them always. The works I have done, you shall do also, and even greater works than these, as faith in yourself and in the power of love grows. Nothing is impossible when you live to serve, live from love, and seek the highest ways. Know that your kind efforts in this world, even when the results remain unknown to you, are witnessed and applauded by God and His angels, and will always be rewarded.

There is no need to worry about the future, as everything is falling into place according to the Father's will. Let your heart not be troubled, but let it be filled with faith that God knows the big picture and has the greatest good in mind always. There is no obstacle God can't move, no injustice God can't recycle into a blessing, and no wrong turn God can't correct. There is nothing to fear. Release your fears from the darkest recesses of your being to make space for new light to shine where fear once dwelt. Fear can never serve you or the world, so allow your worries to be replaced with love as My gift unto you. Fear constricts; love shines!

Healing

Your past is coming up now in order to heal once and for all, and direct your path with more clarity toward the future you have been asking for. It is time to release old wounds, toxic patterns, and unforgiveness that have slowed momentum toward your highest destiny. This is a time of deep sacred healing at many levels to bring about a shift in you to a new level of consciousness. It may seem turbulent at times, but the more you trust the process, and don't resist it, the smoother the ride will be.

This is all happening at a collective level as you build new supportive structures of living and being and move closer to the golden age. Remember, your purpose here is to help, heal and purify the world. The full shift will occur when humanity reaches a tipping point of awakened consciousness. As you awaken and heal, those around you are inspired to follow your example.

CassyTully

cassyTully

Live with Joy

Joy holds the magic of the universe. Lighten up, relax and have more fun. We love to see you laugh and play because JOY attunes you to your purest, most divine essence. Your joyful self is your sacred self! We encourage you to be spontaneous and get into the flow of vibrantly charged JOY energy. Live more joyfully, which will allow you to live more peacefully. Pay attention to that which robs you of joy and begin to eliminate that from your reality. Embrace more of that which lifts you up and brings you enthusiasm, exuberance and lightness of being. Joy is inherently healing. Through connecting to joy, you come into sacred union with your true nature, highest state of being and divine will. It is time for you to awaken to greater JOY!

Eternal Light

Angelic Assistance

Dear Ones:

We wish to clarify the angelic role as it relates to humanity. We hear your pleas and cries, but are not allowed to intervene in ways that "magically fix," eradicate or erase your challenges in the human realm. We do not give any human an unfair advantage, and we would not interfere in any way that would not serve your soul's own natural advancement, growth and learning.

We are not allowed to stop the natural consequences of your actions or interfere with natural laws. (Only God/Creator/Source can do this.) We, too, are subject to the laws of cause and effect and all laws of this particular universe. We cannot take your pain and suffering from you, but we can bear it with you, so you do not have to bear it alone. It breaks our hearts to see you in pain, as we are highly empathic beings, so your pain becomes our pain.

We are permitted to place signs and symbols on your path. We can lead you to the tools that help you heal yourself, overcome your struggles, and meet your challenges in new ways. We spark ideas, insights, and creative ways of looking at situations that allow you to get unstuck from where you are and help you move in a better direction.

We are allowed to give you a push, to give you guidance, to show you signs when you are on the right path, and signs when you are not. The rest is up to you. You have free will to choose your way forward. Many of you heed our advice, and many others ignore it. Oftentimes, you second guess what you are receiving from us and overthink it! We become frustrated and disappointed ourselves by your resistance to our help! We cannot enable you. We cannot do the work for you. We cannot give you the answers, but we can show you where to look to find them for yourselves. We can point you in the right direction, but it is you who must climb the mountain.

We cannot give you the lottery numbers (we get this request a lot), and we never predict or foretell the future, because your future is of your own making by the decisions and choices you make, and we are not to interfere with the pace and path of your progress. We do all we can to guide you, to cheer you on, and to surround you with love and light wherever you go. We give you encouragement and helpful hints along the way to keep you moving forward. We drop the "breadcrumbs" on your path, but it is you who chose to follow or to find your own way. You never walk alone.

We never judge you. Judgment is purely a human thinking process that tends to slow down the momentum of grace in this reality. At our level of being, we bypass this primitive line of thinking. We are not subject to the many human thinking errors that have distorted the way you see the world you live in. We see beyond all mistakes, all judgments, all fears. We behold all before us through the clarity of the lens of love, and we reside and exist within the purest vibration of that love. There is nothing there to fear, judge or question here from our perspective. All is perfect just as it is.

It is difficult to watch you judge yourselves so harshly, and punish yourselves with your own actions, emotions and choices. We acknowledge how difficult it is to live in such a complex reality and we admire you greatly, for you chose this. You chose to come here to learn and to grow. We chose to come here as your watchers, guides and protectors, for as we witness you within this framework, we also learn and grow. We pick you up and dust you off when you fall, as a mother holds and nurtures her injured child, until it is ready to return to the playground and be a part of the game again. And this, dear ones, is a game of your choosing. You can step out temporarily for a rest, and then jump right back in and resume when you are ready!

Our role has been widely misinterpreted and misunderstood. We hope you now have better understanding of how we engage with you, beloveds. We cannot change what you face, encounter, or choose, but we assist you from the sidelines as much as we possibly can without taking over. We wish we could do more, but this is your journey, and at the end you will feel such a sense of accomplishment to have made it through one of the toughest reality frameworks that exist in the time-space matrix and beyond. Think of this as a marathon, and we are the crowd cheering you on. We are the first aid station. We are the water stops. You can quit or give up if you choose, but the satisfaction of seeing it through, and completing what you started, is the sweet reward! You would not have chosen this if you didn't know you were fully capable of reaching the finish line! We wait for your arrival with open arms!

CassyTully

cassyTully

Mother Mary – Queen of Angels

I feel your suffering as if it was my own, my child, for I am your beloved mother. I stay with you through the dark night, I guide your heart through the fear to where peace dwells. The path is twisted and the road can get rugged; in some places it may seem almost impassible. I carry you here. I hold you like the child of God you are. If you only knew that it is impossible to stumble, or slip and fall, as I carry you forward over the jagged stones, the twisted roots, and the highest precipice. I have you. If only you understood how tenderly and lovingly I hold you close to my own heart and carry you through without any help on your part, you would stop the struggle and surrender into your mother's loving arms now. Let me carry you now, my child. I will set you down again when you are ready and guide you by the hand when we reach the other side of this bumpy and dangerous road. I have you now, and that is all you need to know. A mother's intercessions are all-powerful, a mother's prayers are always heard, and a mother's heart is always filled with unconditional love.

Balance

Where are you out of balance? What areas of your life feel disproportionately heavy to you right now? What specifically is weighing you down? Now is the time to let go and surrender this heaviness to God so you can realign your life with greater balance, ease and harmony. There is no one other than you who is insisting that you carry this burden alone for another day. We wish to take it from you now so you can feel much lighter. You always have choice and free will about what you cling to.

As you surrender the heaviness you've been carrying, you will become aware of new opportunities. From this sense of greater balance, lightness and ease will arise, giving clarity and awareness as to what comes next. Trust that you are guided in moving forward. Please do not ignore the signs and the "red flags" we send to guide you toward your highest destiny. We will reveal what you need to know, precisely as you need to know it. You are not given too much at once, because we do not want to confuse or overwhelm you. No need to overthink things! We always help and guide you to make the right choice to support your soul's growth.

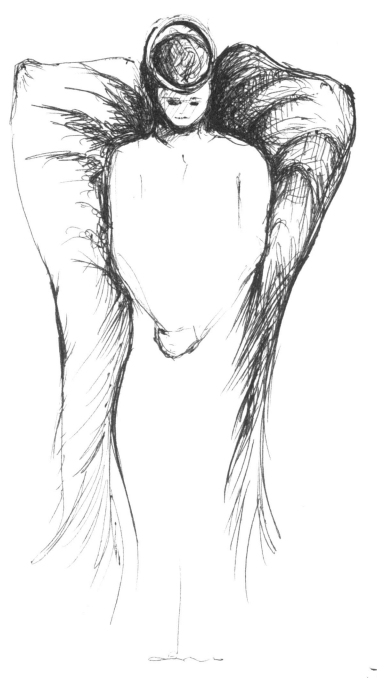

cassy Tully

Love

CassyTully

Hardships

You did not to come to this world to avoid difficulties and struggles, but to learn and grow from them. We are there with you in your darkest moments, filled with awe, compassion and highest admiration for your strength and courage. Even when you didn't see challenges coming, we saw them in advance and prepared you in ways you may one day realize. We are always there, helping you though the darkest hours, leading you always back to the light. We are always sending messages, signs and signals of comfort and peace, to let you know that you never walk through your challenges alone. We are always there, cheering you on, lending you the strength and support you need to rise to the challenge and transform your hardships into hallelujahs! Every hardship raises your consciousness to the next level if you trust in the process and have faith in yourself and all the love around you! You came here to rise!

Abundance

Dance with grace and watch all the pieces fall into place! Celebrate the abundance you have created and are receiving now and give thanks. The abundance is evidence of the power of positive thoughts and faith coming together and showing up in your life. Your successes, victories and joys are evidence of the positivity you have been generating. As you celebrate and give thanks for these blessings, they will continue to increase in form. All things are possible with your conscious participation, along with the grace of God. Trust in the unlimited abundance of spirit. It is only when you doubt and focus on fears that you lose your footing, and the pieces become scattered by your own scattered energy.

When you fall into comparison, envy and judgment, you become disempowered as a conscious co-creator. Remember, these are just illusions. They are not real. Dismiss them now. We angels are your allies to help you manifest your highest destiny. We are constantly sending signs that let you know what your next steps are. Stay open and pay attention to the signs and messages we bring you. We wish an increase of miracles, abundance and blessings in every area of your life.

CassyTully

Cassy Tully

Uncertainty

You may find your lives in a place of uncertainty right now. Uncertainty can seem uncomfortable. In a cosmic sense, but uncertainty is simply a universal pause. Uncertainty is not unlike the pause after the in-breath that happens just before the out-breath. Uncertainty is simply an "intermission" before the "next act" to allow you to have choice. You get to decide what you will keep in your life and what you will release with the out breath. Look at uncertainty as an opportunity to truly reflect upon your current situation and choose what you want. The illusion during times of uncertainty is that you are helpless or stuck. In reality, times of uncertainty are the most potent and powerful times of all. You are given an extended moment to contemplate, think out of the box, think things through, and create what you truly want. Let go of all of the angst around your uncertainty, and take this opportunity to envision what you want and see the way forward to the life you truly desire. Uncertainty can literally be translated into "possibility" if you open to it rather than resist it.

Energy

Humans are also beings of energy who each subtly impact the energetic field of planet Earth. By holding a loving, gentle and peaceful vibration, you systematically raise the vibration of the world around you. We ask that you shine out positivity, love and light in all directions, like the sunshine, and you will positively affect the outcome of these trying times. You have the power of free will to decide what you will bring into your field of energy, which has a profound impact on what you radiate out to the world. Choose wisely. May you be empowered to bring forth to this world the love from whence you came.

Cassy Tully

Mercy

cassyTully

Simplicity

Approach all of life from a higher place, allowing wisdom to rise above the inner chatter of your thoughts and the outer chatter of the world. This small change will allow you to perceive with more clarity, insight and truth. Truth is always found in simplicity, not through noise, chaos and clutter. Wisdom is in simplicity. Solutions and answers are always found in the simplest truths. Contemplate your life and your world with simplicity, from a place of peace and ease. This allows a clarity to help you attune to and receive the divine wisdom and guidance constantly coming through to you.

Truth

You have been asking for the truth to be revealed, but as the truth is made known, you disdain the honesty! As you allow your ears and hearts to remain open, even to challenging truths, you make way for a beautiful new future to emerge where you no longer carry the burdens of deceit and denial. The truth is required for your world to move forward, and to set you free from dishonesty and hidden agendas. These are now being exposed and toppled one by one as light shines into the darkest places. Wake up, breathe, and have patience as God's plan unfolds. Beneath all the falsehoods, evidence of the loyal heart will surface. Where mistrust and doubt have prevailed, there will emerge a faithful servant. No matter what the circumstances appear to be, have faith that your God keeps all promises, and that you are eternally loved and protected.

Remain in faith and trust in this world of conditions. Be loyal in spirit as the the divine plan unfolds. You can celebrate in advance as truth is ushered in. What has been prayed for is now manifesting in ways you will come to understand.

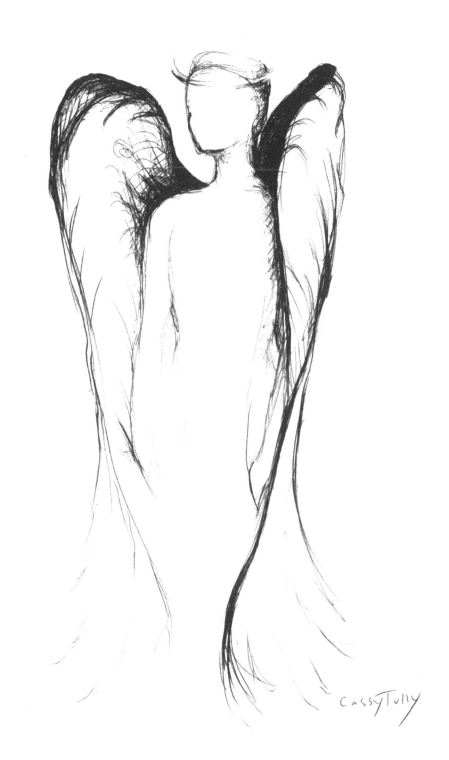

Manifestation

We wish to talk to you today about manifestation, or having the things and experiences you desire to show up in your life. We see how perplexed you are about why your desires do not always manifest the way you want, or seem to get hung up in time and space. We wish to clarify how this happens and how to remedy this situation.

Why aren't my dreams and desires showing up in my life. What is holding them up? What is stopping them?

From our perspective, what we see is that your dreams and desires are NOT only yours. Other people have their own powerful dreams and desires that involve you, too. Any time your dreams and desires for yourself conflict in any way with the dreams and desires of others for you, this creates a hang-up with momentum. Their manifestation energy can jam up yours if they are working in opposition. For example, if you desire a career change, but your partner feels more secure with you maintaining your present job for his or her own reasons, they may stagnate the energy of your forward momentum of career change particularly if they are a strong manifestor and have a strong energetic influence. Many folks are powerful energy workers and don't even know the realm of influence they have on a person or situation.

If you have a very strong desire, it is important to be conscious of who you share your desire with. Some people will energetically work with you to help you manifest it, and other people, who don't want what you do, will energetically work against you, whether they are conscious of it or not. Do not share your desires with people who will not support your dreams and desires. Be very mindful of who you are sharing your intentions with. Most of you share your intentions with little thought of the possibility that someone will counter your energy in ways that can delay and detour your results.

Manifestations are increased, multiplied and energized by each and every person who is in alignment with your intention. If your intention requires others to be on board, like friends and family, it is important to get them in alignment with your desire so you do not have to overcome their opposing energy. Do not share your desires with anyone who would not want to see you succeed, someone who would be envious, or competitive, or someone who wants you to fall rather than rise.

How to be a powerful manifestor:

Some of this is actually a gift. Some of you are born creators and builders who turn thoughts and ideas into things with ease. Everyone has their own strengths and gifts, and everyone has the power to create and manifest. Those of you who have a way of always getting what you want are more energetically aligned at manifesting your energy into things. If you manifest with such ease, it is important for you to be careful what you create for and in the lives of those around you. You do not want to force your own choices on them if they do not choose it. Do not override their free will or there will be a price to pay for doing so for your own selfish reasons.

Manifesting for the greater good is most often about alignment. Your desire must be in alignment with God/Creator/Source/Universe, The more pure you are about your intent, and the less it is ego driven, the more you are a force for good. It is always right to use manifestation principles for that which is in alignment with the highest good of yourself and others. This is not a selfish endeavor. When you become excited about your desires, even passionate about them, there is great forward momentum. We do not mean becoming obsessed with your manifestation, but to decide what you would like to come forward in your life, and then get busy doing something else and let the universe decide how it will come to be. When you become too preoccupied with your manifestation, and try too hard, you get in the way of the momentum already in place.

Be careful you aren't someone who gets in a pattern of sabotaging your own desires. Some of you are afraid of having your dreams come true! You must believe you are worthy and deserving and be willing to receive. Stop second guessing your desire and doubting its validity. This is the basic framework or operating mode of manifestation. This perhaps sounds complicated, but when you are in alignment with desire, it moves forward like a well-aimed arrow making its way towards the target.

Cassy Tully

Progress

cassyTully

Soul Growth

You have arrived. Welcome to the vibration of love and grace. You have come even further than you realize, and have made great strides to get where you are now. These times are about opening to more love and being an expanded version of the love you are. The more love you allow yourself to experience, the more love you have to give. Do more listening and speaking from a place of love. Let love fuel the steps you will take from here forward. If you don't love something, then it is not for you. This is a time of stepping into bigger shoes, and stepping into higher expressions of yourselves. The energies that are dominant now will cause you to really sift out or shake out anything you have been holding onto that is not for your soul's highest good.

New truths are to be revealed in our lives and in our world so you may step up in higher ways to create something better. This is a time of quickening, of rapid soul growth, of reorganizing at every level. Recognize that everything in your life is an opportunity to grow. Hanging on to old patterns, self-defeating habits, and ways of being not conducive to your soul's growth and expansion may cause unnecessary struggle, discomfort and frustration.

As truths are unveiled, practicing acceptance, non-clinging, and letting go will be the keys to rising above. Like a hot air balloon as sandbags are dropped, you will rise to the current of grace. There, you will find your way with ease to new and glorious places to live life from a higher perspective. Finding balance will be especially important at this time. Creativity, time in solitude, time in nature, time by the water, are all ways to regain balance. There is no doom and gloom in store for you. Everything is opportunity at this time: to grow more, to love more and to shine more. Let the light of love lead the way as you navigate these new and glorious times.

cassyTully

Lightworkers

Don't hold back your light for another day. Any moment or area in which you are holding back love, joy, truth, grace, peace and ease of being is a snare in which your soul is trapped. You are the captive and the captor. Only you can release yourself! Your soul was created to be and project the highest and brightest version of you in this world. As you shine the world shines. It is not peculiar to shine brightly, for your creator made you for this very purpose. You have nothing to fear from shining brightly. We angels are the "bodyguards" of the light workers who came to create a better world. You never would have agreed to this earth assignment if you weren't guaranteed and promised our protection. Our advice to you this year is to lighten your load, eliminating all coming between you and your inner light. Don't shrink back from shining as brightly as you can, when you have a team around you cheering you forward and protecting you every step of the way. Don't underestimate the power of YOU to make the world brighter.

Darkness

We ask that you use the longest and darkest days to go within and excavate the darkest parts of yourself. Go deep into in the inner catacombs you have refused to explore, and shine the light of awareness into your own dark spaces. Prepare for the last purge of the darker aspects you have kept tucked away and hidden, even from yourself. You have the power to expel your own inner demons, once and for all, to make way for a new freer, lighter, brighter, more joyful life. Don't let your inner blind spots continue to keep new higher possibilities and inroads out of sight and out of reach. Clear inner cobwebs and brighten your life from the inside out! Doing this will help you comfortably align with the higher energies coming into planet Earth now!

Believe

CassyTully

Synchronicity

When you are observing a surge in synchronicity and divine timing taking place in your life, it indicates that you are aligned with your soul's purpose and path. As you are aware of synchronistic events, recognize that these are organized by by divine hands, messages and assurances that you are being divinely guided, protected, and directed as you walk the path of your soul's highest calling.

Energy

You have been in a holding pattern of great cleansing and purification. You have been and will continue to be asked to rid yourself of old paradigms, outmoded thinking, dysfunctional relationships, jobs, and unwholesome patterns of behavior. Your life has been detoxifying to prepare you for the great new energy from which you will be creating, as you move into your divine life purpose. If you choose to cling to the very things that cause your suffering, you will become increasingly uncomfortable, as the energies of these times are not compatible with self-destructive paths, patterns, or limited ways of thinking, living and being.

You may have noticed yourself going through a phase of remembering, recalling, and processing your past experiences in order to finally release them and heal. This has been a time to clean out your pipes! You are experiencing an energetic reset! The next phase will be about starting over and creating from a new, cleaner, lighter human operating system. You are upgrading. Many of you have been recently, or will be, called into something different, so letting go of the past and old ways is essential. Others will be called to continue to do the same things they have been doing before, but to do them in different ways. It will be obvious which one you are being invited to do. Simply allow new blessings to emerge through you. You will be inspired to be a contribution, rather than a competition, in this higher level of existence. We are observing some of your paving the way for this already, in awe of these positive changes. Change will be the easiest for those who offer the least resistance. Those who refuse and resist are their own stumbling blocks, and will feel stuck and even left behind. Don't look back; keep looking forward with faith that your life and world will continue to get better and better if you are willing to accept the gifts that grace is bringing.

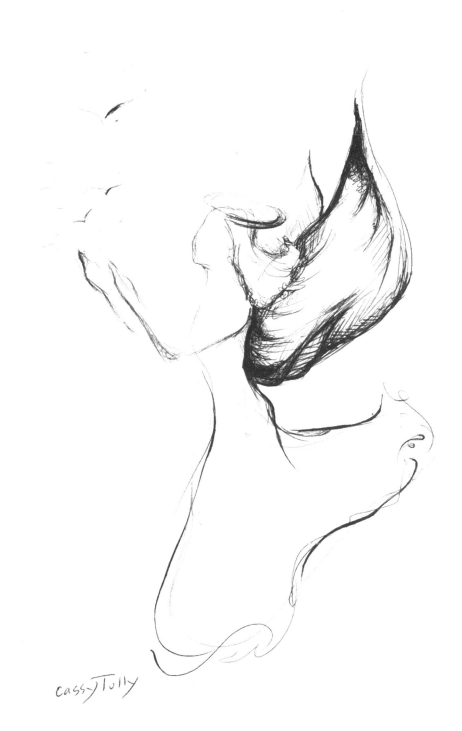

cassyTully

Cassy Tully

Purpose

Throughout time, God has always used the most unlikely persons to accomplish His work. You are no different. There is nothing to fear. Your many prayers about your purpose have rung loudly throughout the heavens. God makes no mistakes. Trust that you will be divinely led. One does not have to be conscious of God's hand for His will to be accomplished. Rest assured, God's will never goes undone. Your continued prayers are always welcome! Trust us when we tell you that all is unfolding by God's design. Your prayers are often answered in unexpected ways, because God sees from a perspective higher than your own. Humans see from their experiences and ideas, but God sees the unseen, and knows the unknown and reveals more as you are ready.

Glory

CassyTully

Answers

You already know, but you have been convinced otherwise and someone else is always "more right" than you. But it is YOU who know. Once you release the desperation to know from someone or something else, the answers will come. Most of you are aware that God (Creator, Source, Great Spirit) is in everything, but you often forget that same Source is in you too... this IS the source of all answers and knowledge. It is available to you at any time. Because you have been convinced that the answers are outside of you, you keep searching futilely, going round and round, looking in the wrong places. You will not find answers there. Do not look up for answers, do not look out. Your heart knows the answers. Your heart FEELS the answers. It is your GPS, and this is why is is located exactly in the center of your being. It points the way like a compass.

Answers don't come from logic of mind; they come from love of heart. The truth always resides in the answers and solutions that come from the space of love within. You stay in confusion only because you try to obtain answers from the places where they do not exist: the mind, the world. By finding them inside you begin to project them into your reality. You project the stepping stones. You project the ladder. You project the scaffolding. You manifest the answers from the inside out, not the outside in. When you attempt this in reverse, confusion and stagnation set in. You cannot move forward by going in reverse.

How do you find the answers within? First, ask the right questions. Know what you are seeking and you will find it. This is why Jesus specifically said, "Seek and you shall find." If you don't know what you are looking for, you will overlook the answers. You will overlook the obvious. Asking brings clarity. After you ask, relax, and get busy with something else. When you stop trying (which is transmitting), you allow yourself to become the receiver. Like an antenna, you draw or attract the answers to your questions from within, like drawing a cat from under a bed. Ignoring the cat and getting busy with something else allows the cat to emerge on its own when ready. When you try to make the cat come out, it goes deeper into hiding, more stubborn and determined than ever to be illusive.

This is very important: When the answers come, PAY ATTENTION. Know the answer when you see it! Be aware that the answer (the lightbulb) you have been seeking is present. (The cat has emerged from under the bed.) Second, BELIEVE. If you do not believe and trust in the answers that come, they will fade, and you fall back into confusion. This is why Jesus emphasized the power and importance of faith and believing.

When you get the same message three times, this is your confirmation. This is why first you will get the answer from within, and then you will have it confirmed in your reality by hearing, reading or seeing the same answer again in close proximity to the time in which you became aware of it. This is because you project that answer into your outer reality to help you see it with greater ease and clarity. Many of you still continue to ignore or fall into disbelief. This is akin to ignoring the GPS in your car and going a different way, taking your own route. You may still get to where you are going, but you may be taking the longer, more winding route and you risk getting lost. For those of you who have done this, do not worry; there is always more than one answer, but we always offer the most direct answer that brings more ease. The concept in your reality to always go with your first answer applies here.

This is the confusing part: Sometimes you will get an answer, which is a step towards the next answer and the next answer. One answer is not always the end all and be all. Often, one answer is given to lead to the next. An answer is not always the final one. We may deliberately give one answer, causing you to stumble upon a better answer, and a better answer and and a better one yet. This is because, you are not ready to receive the best or the full answer, and like a teacher, we lead you step by step to find the right answer for yourself.

You are always more empowered by discovering your own answers, rather than having them spoon-fed. Occasionally will we "hit you over the head" with an answer when you are searching in such a way that you will never find it on your own, but this is rare. We liken your seeking answers to a child on an Easter egg hunt. An adult will tell the child, "colder and colder" or "warmer and warmer," or "hot!"

We often do the same for you, our precious children. However when a child seems to be doing fine on their own, we step back and recognize that they do not need hints. They've got this on their own. They are in the flow. And you, indeed, are here to realize and recognize that flow. You are here to discover and develop your own power and potency. This would never happen if we did it all for you. Be assured that, like the parent hanging in the background at the Easter egg hunt, protectively watching their child discover all the hidden treasures, gifts, surprises and rewards, we are always in the background cheering you on, pulling for you, holding space for you and rooting for your success. No matter how alone you sometimes feel, you are never alone. No one. Not one of you. There is no exception, no matter how pathetic and unlovable you have decided you are. We are at your beck and call, at your disposal and never far away. We watch like a loving, protective parent, allowing you to experiment, because you teach us, you make us proud, and we experience this reality directly through you. We are the Watchers. Just as you watch videos to learn new things, we watch you, with the loving care of a tender and doting parent. We serve you because you are a gift to us. You think that we are your guides, but you are truly our guides. We thank you now for courageously showing us the answers too.

Cassy Tully

cassyTully

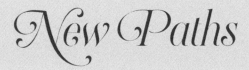

New Paths

We see that many of you are off and running! You are making the changes your soul has been requesting! We are proud of your moving forward towards your soul's calling, and we, too, can feel the newly realized lightness of your path! We will support you and protect you every step of the way, sending signs that we are proud of your courage and your progress! This message is your first sign! Well done!

Peace

Angel Thoughts

Angel Thoughts

Ever since I was a small child, I've had a love for and deep attraction to all things spiritual, mystical and metaphysical, and angels are part of this. By the 6th grade, I had read every book in the library on these mysterious, unseen and unknown subjects. It is no surprise then, that I am the author of seven books (so far) in the mind, body, spirit genre.

I have a master's degree in education, and I teach all things consciousness-raising, awakening and enlightening. I love to assist people in aspiring to their dreams and desires, using their own unique gifts, and honoring their life's true purpose and soul's highest destiny.

After beginning with a prayer, I connect with the angels through telepathy and automatic writing. I have received so many uplifting, comforting and inspiring messages from the angels that I feel called to share them. Besides being an angel communicator and mind/body/spirit wellness teacher, I am an award-winning author, an adept energy healer, animal communicator and overall intuitive. I have been told by the angels that we are all designed and destined to use our "higher senses" in profound ways to serve others and make the world a better place, but we have forgotten how. The angels are now gently inviting us to remember our gifts.

As a child of God, created from love and light, I only use my gifts as a force for good, in the purest and highest truth, integrity, love and light. It is my intention, with the help of the angels, to inspire, encourage, empower, enliven and enlighten as I share these powerful messages far and wide.

Elise Cantrell

Creating the drawings for this book felt like a homecoming for me. They're the reader's glimpse into my sketchbook, a personal place rarely seen. It's much like a diary, giving insight into my artistic inspiration, while my paintings share my God-given talent.

I have always been drawn to portraits because of the way they speak to me, or the way the eyes lead me. The simplicity of pen and ink lets my vision for the angels shine through, and my spirit of creativity is evident in their graceful lines. Angels are fleeting, gone in an instant, and the nature of pen and ink captures this fluidly. One line at a time, the angels wrap their wings around us and bring our thoughts and spirit to a place of peaceful empowerment.

Sketching is a healing process, something anyone can do. As long as you have a pen and paper, the angels can guide your creativity as it flows through your hand onto the page.

I felt a sense of calm as I drew and hope each reader experiences the same sensation of being led to an angelic realm where they're protected and nurtured.

It is my goal to honor all those who have supported my passion for art by encouraging those around me. My golf-inspired paintings celebrate iconic courses, and each of my original masterpieces shares my signature relief-painting technique. As with *Coffee Thoughts: Inspiration Sip by Sip*, my first book with Elise, it is my hope that you feel empowered to share your gifts and love with those around you.

Cassy Tully

Made in the USA
Middletown, DE
03 December 2018